Create and Share | Thinking Digitally

Searching Online

By Kristin Fontichiaro

Published in the United States of America by:

CHERRY LAKE PRESS

2395 South Huron Parkway, Suite 200, Ann Arbor, Michigan
www.cherrylakepublishing.com

Series Adviser: Kristin Fontichiaro
Reading Adviser: Marla Conn, MS, Ed., Literacy specialist, Read-Ability, Inc.
Book Designer: Felicia Macheske
Character Illustrator: Rachael McLean

Photo Credits: © Monkey Business Images/Shutterstock.com, 7; © Rido/Shutterstock.com, 13; © Stock Rocket/
Shutterstock.com, 16

Graphics Throughout: © the simple surface/Shutterstock.com; © Diana Rich/Shutterstock.com; © lemony/Shutterstock.com;
© CojoMoxon/Shutterstock.com; © IreneArt/Shutterstock.com; © Artefficient/Shutterstock.com; © Marie Nimrichterova/Shutterstock.
com; © Svetolk/Shutterstock.com; © EV-DA/Shutterstock.com; © briddy/Shutterstock.com; © Mix3r/Shutterstock.com

Library of Congress Cataloging-in-Publication Data

Names: Fontichiaro, Kristin, author. | McLean, Rachael, illustrator.
Title: Searching online / by Kristin Fontichiaro ; illustrated by Rachael McLean.
Description: Ann Arbor, Michigan : Cherry Lake Publishing, 2020. | Series:
 Create and share : thinking digitally | Includes index. | Audience:
 Grades 2-3.
Identifiers: LCCN 2019033452 (print) | LCCN 2019033453 (ebook) |
 ISBN 9781534159082 (hardcover) | ISBN 9781534161382 (paperback) |
 ISBN 9781534160231 (pdf) | ISBN 9781534162532 (ebook)
Subjects: LCSH: Internet searching—Juvenile literature. | Online
 bibliographic searching—Juvenile literature.
Classification: LCC ZA4230 .F663 2020 (print) | LCC ZA4230 (ebook) | DDC
 025.0425—dc23
LC record available at https://lccn.loc.gov/2019033452
LC ebook record available at https://lccn.loc.gov/2019033453

Cherry Lake Publishing would like to acknowledge the work of the Partnership for 21st Century Learning, a Network of Battelle
for Kids. Please visit *www.battelleforkids.org/networks/p21* for more information.

Printed in the United States of America
Corporate Graphics

Table of
CONTENTS

CHAPTER ONE
Searching...4

CHAPTER TWO
Keywords..6

CHAPTER THREE
Understanding Results..............................10

CHAPTER FOUR
Narrowing Your Search............................14

CHAPTER FOUR
Personalized Search and YouTube.........18

GLOSSARY..22
FOR MORE INFORMATION 23
INDEX 24
ABOUT THE AUTHOR 24

Searching

How late is the library open? What causes rainbows? How do you program a robot? We use **search engines** to find answers like these on the internet all the time.

There are many different search engines. The most common are Google and Bing. Some search engines are built into **browsers** like Safari, Chrome, and Internet Explorer. Every browser has a secret **algorithm** that determines the websites you see. That is why the same search in different browsers can give you different results.

Alexa, Siri, and Google Assistant are **digital assistants**. They use search engines to answer questions you ask them. Unlike an online search, these assistants will pick just one answer it thinks is best. When would it be good to get just one answer? When would many answers be better?

Get to Know Your Search Engines

Type **make slime** in your favorite search engine. How many results do you get? How is the information organized? Which results would you click on first?

Now type that again in a different search engine. Do you get the same number of results? Are they organized the same way? Compare the two search engines. Do you prefer using one over the other? Why?

Take a survey. Ask your friends and family which search engine they prefer using. What's their reason behind it?

When we search, we usually get too many answers. In this book, you'll learn tips and tricks to help you find more of what you need and less of what you don't.

CHAPTER TWO

Keywords

A strategy is a tool or clever plan that helps you reach your goal. Smart searchers choose the important words, or **keywords**, that describe what they are looking for. They don't type entire questions.

Using Nouns to Search

Aurora wants to plant sunflowers. But she won't if they will get too tall and block her window. She wants to know, "How tall do sunflowers grow?" The main ideas are **tall** and **sunflowers**.

We could type **tall sunflowers**. Instead, try the noun *height* instead of the adjective *tall*: **height sunflowers**. Nouns are better for searching!

You don't have to type common words like *a, an, the, for, of,* or *my*.

6

Remember, always ask an adult's permission
before searching the internet.

Using Synonyms to Search

Quincy wonders, "What kind of pet is best for my family?" The obvious keywords are *pet* and *family*. But we might search with **synonyms**. He might search *dog* instead of *pet*. Or he might realize that he has a more specific question than he first thought. He doesn't need to know which pet is best for *any* family. He wants a pet for *his* family. He wants a pet that will feel comfortable in an apartment with a tiny yard and a new baby. So he creates searches like these: **apartment pet** or **pet small yard** or **pets children**. He won't know which search will be best until he tries them all.

Search engines are getting better at helping you if you spell words wrong. But if you don't get the results you expect, ask someone to help you spell your keywords. You never have to type capital letters or punctuation when you search.

Writing Keywords

Practice turning these questions into keywords. Can't think of any keywords? Imagine you have found the perfect website with the answer on it. What words would be on that page? Those are your keywords. Remember that sometimes, the right keyword isn't the exact word in your question—it's a synonym!

- Where will the 2028 Olympics be?
- How old is President George W. Bush?
- How do you play Red Rover?
- What are some foods in Germany?
- How far away is the Philippines?

Red rover, red rover, send...

CHAPTER THREE

Understanding Results

When you search, you get a list of possible websites as results. Each website is a hit. It's tempting to click the first hit right away. Try taking a moment to review the results instead.

Go back and study the results from your **make slime** search. The blue underlined words are **hyperlinks,** or links for short. Click on a link to go to that site.

Below each hyperlink is a **snippet** of text with a description. Read the snippet before you click. If it looks too complicated or like it is talking to adults, choose a different result.

Search engines sometimes guess what information you need and give it to you in a box on the results page. For example, search the name of your favorite movie. You will probably get a box with basic information about it as part of your results.

Helpful vs. Not Helpful Sites

Type in **basketball rules** in your search engine. Find the two most and least helpful sites.

This is what we picked:

MOST HELPFUL	LEAST HELPFUL
YouTube—Basketball Basics for Kids **Reason:** Video was easy to understand.	Ducksters—Basketball: The Center **Reason:** Only contained information about the center position.
Kiddle—Basketball Facts for Kids **Reason:** Information was broken up in a way that was easy to read.	UPMC Children's Hospital of Pittsburgh—Basketball Safety Tips **Reason:** Information was only about staying safe while playing basketball.

Your turn! What were the two most and least helpful sites you picked? What were your reasons?

Do you think the best way to learn about the rules of basketball is from text, images, or video?

What search engine do you use most often?

CHAPTER FOUR

Narrowing Your Search

Let's say you're studying President Gerald R. Ford. You want to know more about when he was a kid in Michigan. So you search for **ford michigan**. Your results aren't what you wanted! You got results about Ford car dealerships in Michigan, the Ford Motor Company in Michigan, Ford Field for football, and more. There are a lot of things named Ford in Michigan.

What do you do? You need to be more specific. Here are some things you could try.

1. Add search terms like **president** or **gerald**. This is better, but you still get results for buildings named after him.

2. Put quotation marks around his name. Try **"gerald ford"** and then try the search with **"gerald r. ford"**. Often, people don't use middle names or initials when they write about someone. So searching for his name with and without his middle name or initial helps widen your search!

3. After brainstorming with your school librarian, you decide to add **childhood** to the search term.

4. Your final search is **"gerald ford" michigan childhood** and **"gerald r. ford" michigan childhood**. Success! You find the information you were looking for.

Look at the top of the results page for other search choices. Click *Maps* to see where things are or how far apart they are. Click *Images* to see just photos and drawings. Click *Videos* to see only video results.

What would you like to learn more about?

Search Further

There is another famous Ford in Michigan: Henry Ford, the automobile manufacturer. Start with the same search: **ford michigan**. Then write out some possible keyword searches. Adjust your search until all the results are about Henry Ford's house. Then click on *Maps* to see where the house was. Click *Images* to see photos of it. And click *Videos* to find a tour of the house.

Detroit, Michigan

CHAPTER FIVE

Personalized Search and YouTube

Personalized Search

Many search engines and browsers track your location and what you have searched for before. Your results are based on what they think they know about you.

This **personalized** search can be helpful. If you search **mcdonald's**, personalized results might show the one closest to you. Did you use National Geographic for your animal research recently? Then that site might show up higher in your results next time.

Sometimes, personalization causes new problems, like when people search for news. The search engine will know if you mostly click on Fox News, which has a **conservative** focus. Over time, it might show you mainly conservative news. You might miss stories that explain how other people are thinking about an issue. The same is true if you click on more **liberal** stories. Over time, you would see more liberal news and fewer conservative voices. When we don't see balanced points of view, it is hard to be a good citizen.

Try your browser's **incognito mode**. (Ask your librarian or an adult for help! Finding the incognito mode is different with each browser.) It won't personalize your results. It can be helpful to compare results from a normal search with those you get in incognito mode. You can also use duckduckgo.com as your search engine. It does not collect personal information or do personalized searches.

YouTube

Video is a great way to learn how to do things. Many people search YouTube instead of a browser when they only want video results. There is a lot of great stuff there to help you learn, enjoy music, and celebrate events. YouTube is owned by Google, so the same keyword strategies work there. But you can't see snippets or a preview like you can with website results. So you need to be careful when deciding which videos to watch.

Teaching Others

Now you know the tips and tricks on how to search the internet effectively. Share them with others!

Here are the ideas we talked about in this book:

- Type keywords, not an entire question or sentence.
- Turn adjectives such as *tall* into nouns like *height*.
- Don't include short, common words.
- Don't use capital letters or punctuation.
- Use your best spelling.
- Use quotation marks around the exact words you want to see in your results.
- Read the snippets before you click.
- Click on *Maps*, *Images*, and *Videos* to see if there is more information you can learn.
- Search in incognito mode to see more points of view.
- Tell an adult if you find weird or confusing videos.

Can you come up with a creative way to teach others about what you've learned? Maybe you can team up with a friend and start a **podcast**. Or you can create a quick video **tutorial** on YouTube. How about a poster?

GLOSSARY

algorithm (AL-guh-rih-thum) computer code that makes decisions

browsers (BROU-zurz) programs that connect you to the internet, such as Chrome, Safari, Firefox, or Internet Explorer

conservative (kuhn-SUR-vuh-tiv) a political view that values small government

digital assistants (DIJ-ih-tuhl uh-SIS-tuhntz) internet-connected devices that you command with your voice to get answers, turn on music, set alarms, tell you jokes, and more

hyperlinks (HYE-pur-lingk) a piece of text on a website that is linked to another

incognito mode (in-kahg-NEE-toh MOHD) a way to search without getting personalized results

keywords (KEE-wurdz) the words you type in a search bar

liberal (LIB-ur-uhl) a political view that values change

personalized (PUR-suh-nuhl-ized) search results that are based on where you are and what you have looked for before

podcast (PAHD-kast) a program over the internet for people to listen to on a computer, tablet, or smartphone

search engines (SURCH EN-jinz) software programs that look online for information that matches your keywords and past history

snippet (SNIP-pit) a few words from a web page that are listed in your search results

synonyms (SIN-uh-nims) words that mean the same or nearly the same thing

tutorial (too-TOR-ee-uhl) a short course that teaches you about something

BOOKS

Green, Sara. *Google*. Minneapolis, Minnesota: Bellwether Media, 2016.

Lindeen, Mary. *Smart Online Searching: Doing Digital Research*. Minneapolis, Minnesota: Lerner, 2016.

WEBSITES

Common Sense Education—5 Must-Have Google Search Tips for Students
https://www.commonsense.org/education/articles/5-must-have-google-search-tips-for-students
Learn even more tricks for finding what you need online!

DuckDuckGo
https://duckduckgo.com
This search engine does not collect personal information, like location and online behavior, or do personalized searches.

INDEX

Alexa, 4
algorithms, 4
assistants, digital, 4

Bing, 4
browsers, 4, 18, 19

Chrome, 4

digital assistants, 4
duckduckgo.com, 19

Google, 4, 20
Google Assistant, 4

hyperlinks, 10–11

incognito mode, 19
Internet Explorer, 4

keywords, 6–9, 20

nouns, 6

personalization, 18–21
points of view, balanced, 19

quotation marks, 14

Safari, 4
search engines, 4–5, 8

searching, online, 4–5
  narrowing search, 14–17
  personalized results,
    18–21
  understanding results,
    10–13
Siri, 4
snippets, 11
synonyms, 8

video, 20

websites, 4, 10

YouTube, 20

About the AUTHOR

Kristin Fontichiaro teaches at the University of Michigan School of Information and writes books for adults and kids. She loves black cherry soda and searching online.